Robert Graves

by GEORGE STADE

 Columbia University Press
NEW YORK & LONDON 1967

COLUMBIA ESSAYS ON MODERN WRITERS is a series of critical studies of English, Continental, and other writers whose works are of contemporary artistic and intellectual significance.

Editor: William York Tindall

Advisory Editors

Jacques Barzun   W. T. H. Jackson   Joseph A. Mazzeo   Justin O'Brien

Robert Graves is Number 25 of the series.

GEORGE STADE is Assistant Professor of English at Columbia University.

Acknowledgment is made to Mr. Robert Graves, A. P. Watt and Son, and Cassell and Company, Ltd., for permission to quote from Graves's works and to the following: The Hogarth Press, for selections from *The Feather Bed, Mock Beggar Hall,* and *The Marmosite's Miscellany;* William Heinemann, Ltd., for selections from *Fairies and Fusiliers, Whipperginney,* and *Poems, 1926–1930;* Faber and Faber and Farrar, Straus, and Giroux for selections from *The White Goddess;* and Collins-Knowlton-Wing for selections from *Collected Poems, 1955* (copyright © 1955 by International Authors, N.V.), *New Poems, 1962* (copyright © 1961, 1962 by International Authors, N.V.), *Man Does, Woman Is* (copyright © 1963, 1964 by International Authors, N.V.), *Love Respelt* (copyright © 1965, 1966 by International Authors, N.V.), and *Collected Poems, 1966* (copyright © 1966 by International Authors, N.V.).

Robert Graves

Robert Graves is a minor poet of major proportions. In 1958 he estimated that up to then he had written close to five million words. He has since published another twenty books. A list of his first editions would include over one hundred and thirty items. Among them are fifteen novels; a dozen books of criticism; as many volumes of biography and studies in myth and history; a dozen collections of short fiction and other miscellaneous writings; a half-dozen editions of other writers' poems, letters, ballads, nursery rhymes; translations from Greek, Latin, French, Spanish, German; a travel book; books for children; a handbook on English prose; a study of swearing and improper language; a book on dreams; and a couple of plays. He has published 824 poems that I know of. Most of them have come out in thirty-nine successive collections. Only three of these books are dull.

But though he is a prolific, an imitated, and since 1926 a consistently good poet, he is not a major one, by choice, and according to his own definition of "major." "Minor poetry, so called to differentiate it from major, is the real stuff," says Graves. The work of a major poet, let us say, is a system of weights and measures through the use of which we can determine the character and value of other poetry. Poetry written immediately subsequent to his can most intelligibly be talked about with reference to his work; poetry contemporary with his can subsequently be understood best with reference to his work. A major poet is himself a tradition, a system of coordinates by means of which we locate other poetry in literary space. Graves claims that he is a traditional poet, as he is, but he is not himself a tradition, as, say, Chaucer, Shakespeare, Pope, and Eliot are, nor does he want to be.

But that is exactly what a number of his critics, starting with Edwin Muir, and swelling to a chorus during the fifties, have been claiming for him. Robert Graves, according to these critics, is now the most important poet writing in English and the best model for young poets seeking either to establish a new tradition or to recover the native one that "Franco-American modernism," as he calls it, is supposed to have set aside. With regard to the native tradition and "the foul tidal basin of modernism," Graves states the case with less qualification than his critics, but he has not accepted their claim that he is a "major" poet, nor has he tried to write like one. And in these refusals lies much of what is unique and valuable about his poetic career.

What Graves has against major poetry is its immensity, of length, theme, conception, or ambition. "The effect of *Paradise Lost* on sensitive readers," says Graves, "is, of course, overpowering. But is it the function of poetry to overpower? To be overpowered is to accept spiritual defeat." Major poems are first of all long poems, his argument goes, and long poems, strictly speaking, do not exist. What we call a long poem, if there is any poetry in it at all, is really a collection of short poems set amidst verse. True poetry is Muse poetry, the product of a trance, and trances are of short duration—spontaneous overflows do not flow for long. "All Muse poetry is minor poetry, if length be the criterion." Long poems, major poems, are the products of will.

And of ambition. The major poet is after either contemporary or posthumous fame. To seek contemporary fame, says Graves, is to make oneself a hostage to public opinion. A poet who writes for the public, "rather than for the Muse—that is to say for poetic necessity," has forsaken his first professional

[4]

virtue, his integrity, which "consists in his not forming ties that can impair critical independence, or prevent him from telling the whole truth about anything, or force him to do anything out of character." The man who would be a true poet should share the sentiment that Graves communicated to his BBC audience: "Frankly, honest Public, I am not professionally concerned with you, and expect nothing from you." The truth of the matter is that "a poet needs no public."

The major poet who seeks contemporary fame is also a *Zeitgeist* poet, a man who tries to capture the spirit of the times in verse, and therefore writes only what Graves calls posthumous poems; by the time the poem is written the times have changed. The *Zeitgeist* poet also violates the poet's second virtue, sincerity, which consists in his not writing about anything he has not personally and directly experienced. A poet, like any other man, is affected by the times in which he lives, but "what matters is the degree to which a poet can transcend his period." Further, the *Zeitgeist* poet, according to Graves, is neither a person nor, as advertised, impersonal. Graves has always insisted both that poetry is private, the expression of a unique personality's unique experiences, and that the source of true poetry is above, beyond, or below the poet's ego. From about 1917 to 1925, under the influence of W. H. R. Rivers, a psychologist, and the romantic critics, Graves thought that poems were precipitated by an internal conflict of which the poet's conscious mind was unaware. In 1926 he began, with Laura Riding's help, to develop the theory that poems came out of a transpersonal universe of absolute value. And in 1944 he discovered what he has held to since, that poems come out of a mythic system of themes and symbols to which the poet is led by an unqualified love of the Muse. The relation of integrity and sincerity to all this is that the poet can only discover what is not himself if he is exactly and nothing but himself. The *Zeit-*

geist poet is no one and everyone; he "enlarges his public figure at the expense of the private self."

To write for posterity is even worse, because then the poet is addressing a public whose tastes he cannot hope to predict. "To invoke posterity is to weep on your own grave." But Graves does not often waste sympathy on poets who in his estimation have written out of ambition. His essays on Vergil, Milton, Pope, and Wordsworth, Graves's favorite examples of past careerists, and his remarks on such contemporaries as Eliot, Pound, Stevens, Thomas, Auden, Yeats, and Williams are properly a scandal. "What is wrong with Robert Graves?" wrote Edith Sitwell. "He has now insulted, and very grossly, almost every poet of our time." Up until about 1926 Graves used to say that what was wrong with him was what was wrong with everybody in those "goddawful" postwar years. But he then decided that whatever the truth of the matter, it was more fruitful for him to consider himself right, and the rest, who were trying to write "major poems of truly contemporary malaise," wrong. Because of their wrongs, "careerism is the plague of contemporary poetry." And since 1929, when he wrote his autobiography—"a formal goodbye to you and to you and to me and to all that"—and set sail for Majorca (where he has lived since), Graves, determined to be neither a careerist, a major poet, nor an embodiment of the *Zeitgeist*, has defined his professional role as that of being the poet who was estranged not only from the twentieth century and his country but from the projects and practices of the poets of that time and that place as well.

This deliberate and contentious estrangement, along with his equally deliberate and contentious choice of models—Skelton, Jonson, Elizabethan lyrics, traditional ballads, broadsides, nursery rhymes, Keats, Christina Rossetti, Hardy, Housman, de la Mare, and the medieval Welsh poets—has given his verse a

[6]

number of characteristics that can be opposed point by point to modernist ones. Graves, for example, stresses sincerity, rather than impersonality; emotion and suggestiveness, rather than the exact rendering of perceptions; the automatic and unconscious element in composition, rather than skill and craftsmanship; the concatenation of images and themes by association, rather than by juxtaposition; euphony, rather than words charged with meaning through sound; harmony, rather than dissonance; personal variations on existing metrical schemes, rather than the use of "absolute rhythm," which is based on the notion that "a new cadence means a new idea"; common-sense reality, rather than distortion; illustrative imagery, rather than the numinous symbol or the opaque image; what words "mean," rather than what they are; the common word, rather than the exact one, no matter how uncommon; "country sentiment," rather than metaphysical wit or urban funk; the perspectives of children, primitives, madmen, and dreamers, as tidied up by the superego, rather than either the chill irony of the mature critical intelligence or the libidinous rage of adult and civilized depravity; the idea that poetry gratifies, heals, pleases, rather than the idea that in one sense poetry forces us through pain to re-create ourselves, but that in another, "poetry makes nothing happen"; intuition, rather than erudition; the problem of reconciling tastes created by the tradition of English poetry with personal obsessions, rather than the obsessive need to create new tastes in the process of destroying old ones; love over sex, rather than the triumphs and defeats of an inexorably subversive sexuality; the reality and value of a unique and persisting self that survives sequences of mood and experience, rather than the reality of the fluid or fragmented self, or the value of getting around oneself to either the fields of light or the heart of darkness; and so on.

The irony of Graves's career, then, is that the nature of his work is as much determined by the *Zeitgeist* as that of any poet who, in Graves's phrase, has "turned himself into a period." The tradition he refused to embody is the one by which we understand him.

For all that, I must agree with him that "nothing is better than the truly good, not even the truly great." And his poems, for almost exactly forty years now, have been (with the exception of the self-congratulatory poems that make up about one-quarter of any volume) remarkably and consistently good. But they have been good in a special way. Graves's poems succeed so often because he very seldom tries to do more than he can. We watch him perform not as though he were an acrobat whose every move risked his neck, but as a deft and economical craftsman whose composure comes from an abundance of raw materials and no anxiety about the worth of what he is doing. If in reading his poems we are not drowned in exquisite sensations, as by a symphony, or do not feel our nervous systems restructured, as by moving through a force field, we do get the very real and less tiring pleasure of examining something like an expertly handcrafted piece of glassware of functional rather than decorative style. As we look on we get to feel that each line of the glassware and each figure on its surface has behind it generations of other craftsmen. One is especially grateful for these virtues, I think, because they are so hard to come by, as is Graves's famous lucidity. Because Graves's virtues are those of a minor poet one can approach his work without a grim determination to master it or without anxieties about the adequacy of one's own education, intelligence, or sensibility. This absence of willful obscurity and moral blackmail especially pleased Max Beerbohm. "My joy in him," he said, "is n͞o͞t diminished because he is so intelligible."

On the other hand, when Graves's poems fail, it is because the manifest technical dexterity with the small technical risk and the slightness of content gives them a slippery quality, like a counterfeit coin's. Or they fail because the compulsive eccentricity of attitude and gesture with the conventionality of form makes them cranky, that is, eccentric and conventional at once, like the minor suspects in a British murder mystery. The sameness of the themes, forms, and figures among the poems in any one of Graves's collections wears one down as quickly as the aggressive demands of the modernists. And because his poems are only personal, because he refuses to work out the public relevance of his private obsessions (which are, in any case, of a rather old-fashioned sort), because he never addresses his audience, but only allows it to overhear him, his readers are less likely to mull his poems over, memorize them, make the poems permanent agencies of their un-, semi-, and full consciousnesses. If his poems never make anyone uncomfortable, it is because they never nudge anyone out of whatever complacencies he lives by. And so far they have only appealed to the old, the middle-aged, and the prematurely aged. With regard to the traditional doctrine that poetry is supposed to move, delight, and instruct, we can say that Graves is willing to sacrifice movement and instruction for delight. The question as to whether modern poetry and its readers need more of delight or of the others is still open.

What is not an open question, to me, at least, is whether or not Graves is worth reading, if not imitating. And he has told us how to read him. "A volume of collected poems," he says, "should form a sequence of the intenser moments of the poet's spiritual autobiography, moments for which prose is insufficient." To say that one is reading Graves, then, is not to speak synecdochically; to describe how and what he wrote is to describe how he lived. We can stop for a look at the prose whenever it will help us to fill in the interstices between those intenser moments that are the poems.

[9]

Graves always writes retrospectively about his poems up to *Whipperginney* (1923) with relation to World War I, although some of the poems in *Over the Brazier* (1916) were written while he was still in school. The "emotion underlying" these early volumes, he says, "was a frank fear of physical death." The prewar poems of bucolic coziness, we are to understand, are related to the war by way of contrast; they represent the condition of healthful normality against which the experience of war is to be measured. Another group of poems, those written "in a romantic vein, of wizards, monsters, ghosts and outlandish events and scenes," those on the subject of childhood, and those depicting rural amorousness, "country sentiment," Graves describes as digressive. "The digression was towards wistfulness, in disregard of the pseudo-adult experience of soldiering." In sum, the poems in *Over the Brazier, Goliath and David* (1916), *Fairies and Fusiliers* (1917), *The Treasure Box* (1919), and *Country Sentiment* (1920) are all related to the war by way of confrontation or escape.

As it turned out, Graves had good cause for the frank fear of physical death expressed in the poems of 1914–16. On his twenty-first birthday (July 26, 1916), Graves tells us in his autobiography, *Goodbye to All That* (1929), his "official death occurred." A colonel, looking over Graves's wounds, which had forced his heart out of place and had nearly emasculated him, pronounced Graves dead. After his death had been officially announced, the military confessed a mistake, but Graves demurred: "But I *was* dead, an hour or more" (*Fairies*, 70). And he has never acknowledged his father's claim, based on private and official records, and recorded in *To Return to All That* (1930) (Graves senior's autobiographical reply to *Goodbye*), that the report of his son's death had occurred on another day. "I *did* die on my way down to the field hospital," Graves junior wrote Edward Marsh. One can sympathize with Graves, who as a poet and scholar has always preferred poetic resonance to the dull monotone of facts; and to die on a twenty-first birthday is to illustrate a kind of poetic justice.

Graves came out of the war with mental, as well as physical, trauma. He suffered first a breakdown and then lingering neurasthenia, for which W. H. R. Rivers ("biologist, neurologist, anthropologist, psychologist, a pioneer in every branch of science he undertook," according to Graves) treated him, as he had treated Siegfried Sassoon and Wilfred Owen. The cause of these traumas, the war ("which permanently changed my outlook on life"), Graves came to see as a kind of rite of passage for himself and his generation. War had been "the inward scream, the duty to run mad," and his generation had come out of it dominated by "the death curse in which humanity seems entailed." "We agreed that the world had gone mad," said Siegfried Sassoon, recalling in his autobiography a wartime conversation with Graves.

Graves wanted in his self-absorbed and quixotic way to do what he could for the neurosis at large while he worked on his own, and Dr. Rivers showed him the way. Rivers' theory was that every neurotic system, like dreams, was at once the product of a mental conflict and an attempt to resolve it, and he suggested to Graves that poems were the same. Graves added to this theory the notion that one man's versified resolution would work for another man with a similar conflict. He and his generation had both been shaken loose by conflicts arising out of the experience of warfare, Graves understood, so it seemed reasonable to hope that his poems would restore them; as, he hoped, they would him. "My hope was to help the recovery of public health of mind, as well as my own, by the writing of 'therapeutic' poems," he explained in 1949.

So when he came to write in 1922 his first book of criticism, *On English Poetry*, based on "evidence mainly subjective"—

[11]

that is, the writing of the early poems—Graves advertised poetry as "a form of psycho-therapy" for the neurosis of poets and the culture they express and address. He assured his readers that "a well-chosen anthology is a complete dispensary for the more common mental disorders and may be used as much for prevention as for cure." A poem's rhythm, the argument goes, puts the reader in a hypnotic trance; he is confronted with an allegorical solution of the problem that has been troubling him; his unconscious accepts the allegory as applicable to his own condition; the emotional crisis is relieved—and we have another case of Homeopathic Healing through the Power of Poetry.

The very earliest poems are not much better than the theory. The poems overtly dealing with the war are of various types. There is the war-is-hell type; the type of heroical defiance; the soldierly drinking song; the lament for dead buddies; homesick evocations of the English countryside; and so forth—all marred by immaturity of tone and imitativeness. Other poems recount Graves's loss of Christian faith, his dislike of reason, and his disgust with wartime promiscuity. Underlying all these is a kind of sweet innocence that no one could now imagine coming from a poet in his late adolescence:

> When a dream is born in you
>   With a sudden clamorous pain
> When you know the dream is true
>   And lovely, with no flaw nor stain,
> O then, be careful, or with sudden clutch
> You'll hurt the delicate thing you prize so much.
>
> (*Goliath*, 7)

There is much about love in these poems, but it is all between either fairy personages, or children, or comrades. A number of the poems refer to the "Dick" of *Goodbye*. Graves had an "honorably chaste" crush on this man until about the time he met Nancy Nicholson, who became his first wife.

The poems of escape need only detain us for a minute. These

are about fairy pipers, furry clouds, moonlit ghosts, dying knights, kindly goblins, friendly oaks, frosty nights, and "jolly rascal lads." There are enough vegetables named, from Troll's nosegays to double red daisies to gorse, in any one of these volumes for a gaggle of Georgians. Romping among the blue-bells and brambles are manticors, rocs, unicorns, basilisks, cocatrices, gryphons, bats, cuckoos, dragons, harpies, wyverns, sprites, elves, fauns, fiends, and hippogriffs. Graves, who had first met Edward Marsh in 1913, four years later called him "the Father of Modern English Poetry." Marsh, who liked Graves's poems, "pointed out that they were written in the poetic vocabulary of fifty years ago," Graves confesses. Marsh, one supposes, did not much like such words as "wingle," "dingle," and "frore."

Graves took criticism of this sort to heart. The first poem in *Fairies and Fusiliers* is "To an Ungentle Critic." The poet presents this churl as complaining that there is no "New Age/ Of Poetry in my worn-out words." Must his verse die "stillborn" because "old men/ squeal for something new?" the poet rhetorically asks. No, he will continue in his "knock-kneed" but "classic way."

> And, sir, be careful what you say;
> There are old-fashioned folk still like it.

And in "John Skelton," from the same volume, Graves explains that the classic way is Skelton's way:

> He struck what Milton missed,
> Milling an English grist
> With Homely turn and twist.
> He was English through and through,
> Not Greek, nor French, nor Jew.

Skelton, like Graves, "Rhymes serenely on as English poets should."

Country Sentiment (1920), the last volume of this group

under consideration, is also the best; with *Pier-Glass* (1921) and *Whipperginney* (1923) it was, in fact, the best for some time to come. Recent editions of Graves's *Collected Poems* retain more poems from these three volumes than from the four preceding them and the five published immediately after them put together. Among those retained are not the poems discussed above. The best poems in the second half of *Country Sentiment*, throughout *Pier-Glass*, and in the first half of *Whipperginney* introduce a new note of terror, which is to be distinguished from the "frank fear of physical death" we have noted. All the subjects of the early escape poems—love, childhood, fairyland, the English countryside, poetry itself—become permeated with dreadful presences.

The source of these presences was Graves's war neurosis. By late 1918, when he began writing these poems, his neurasthenia, "sharpened rather than blunted by the experience of peace," had become especially acute. The experience of peace included marriage, into which, Graves tells us, he has gone with insufficient preparation, no amount of which, however, would have enabled him to cope with Nancy Nicholson. That uncompromising feminist turned up at their wedding reception in breeches, kept her maiden name, insisted that their children take her name rather than Graves's, and, he says, "found it difficult not to include me in her universal condemnation of men."

Within fifteen years or so Graves would be arguing Nancy's views on male narrowness, stupidity, and callousness and on the evils of patriarchal dominance, and arguing them with considerable vehemence, but for the time his personal and domestic difficulties improved his love poetry immeasurably. After his marriage there are no more poems of comrades arm in arm, cuddly trolls, and unassigned amorousness. The love poems now deal with the obstacles that love put in its own way. Out

[14]

of his special case Graves adds to these obstacles a frank fear of female sexuality and a sweaty horror of lust. In one poem, Delilah Becker, having stabbed her husband, "Now sits secure," triumphing in her "inward joy," while her poor husband unsuccessfully tries to haunt her (*Pier-Glass*, 53). In another, the murderess throws off her guilt and decides that it was better to have killed than to have forgiven: "Kill, strike, again, again" (*Pier-Glass*, 16).

The terror is everywhere. The religion Graves had so effortlessly thrown off now comes back in the form of ghosts and ghouls who haunt the once friendly countryside, "Greedy of human stuff to snare/ In webs of murk." Nor is an imaginative return to childhood any more comforting. Children are broken down by "ancestral sin" or open their picture books to find nothing but scenes of lust, betrayal, infanticide, and arbitrary bloodshed. In "Down," perhaps the best, and with "The Children of Darkness" the only enigmatic of these poems, an old man who is dying tries to distract his mind by thinking of a childhood experience. He had dropped a stone down a well, allowed his mind to follow it, and waited until his thoughts floated back "From the deep waters." But the distraction does not work; the "simple tales" that puzzled childhood are now "answerless," and his mind sinks "Through mattress, bed, floor, floors beneath, stairs, cellars," until finally

> Light closed up behind him,
> Now stunned by the violent subterrene flow
> Of rivers, whirling down to hiss below
> On the flame axis of this terrible world;
> Toppling down upon their water-fall. . . .

Some "inadvertent motion or word uttered/ Of too-closed-packed-intelligence" had sunk him "Funereally with creeping, down, downed, lost!" (*Pier-Glass*, 36–37)

"Down" brings us to the great theme of these poems, which

is that the mind has mountains, cliffs of fall, no-man fathomed, and labyrinthine passageways, a nightmare at each turning. The mind being such, all of its products, notably poems, are likely to be ghost raddled. In "Ghost Raddled" someone asks for a song, but the poet knows only "clouded tales of wrong/ And terror," of groans, of "demons in the dry well/ That cheep and mutter," of "Blood choking the gutter." How can he sing, he asks, "Do flowers and butterflies belong to a blind December?" (*Sentiment*, 64)

Clearly Graves had reached an impasse. His alternatives were either to stop writing poetry or to write only poems about rotten breasts and sinking minds. He could not stop writing poems any more than he could stop having nightmares. Moreover, he was still convinced that poetry could be therapeutic; one only had to go about writing it in the right way. *On English Poetry*, the 1922 book of criticism, had expressed the hope that if one looked at the monsters long enough the ogres and pygmies would turn into fauns and elves. But the poems we have just finished considering made it clear to Graves that, if apparitions fade before the courageous eye, they soon appear in solider forms and more questionable shapes. What was Graves to do? He would look at what he had to see, he decided, but from a distance, and his perspective would be, of all things, philosophical analysis.

The Author's Note to *Whipperginney* tells us that the volume continues for awhile in the mood of *Pier-Glass*, "but in most of the later pieces will be found evidence of greater detachment in the poet and the appearance of a new series of problems in religion, psychology and philosophy." These later pieces, Graves admits, are "of less emotional intensity." The main intellectual interests in *Whipperginney* are psychological; in *The Feather Bed* (1923) they are mostly psychological and religious; but *Mock Beggar Hall* (1924) "was almost wholly

[16]

philosophical." In *The Winter Owl* (1924), *Welchman's Hose* (1925), and *The Marmosite's Miscellany* (1925), social, political, literary, economic, religious, scientific, and psychological problems are treated philosophically. "Metaphysics soon made psychology of secondary interest for me; it threatened almost to replace poetry," he later said of this period.

But the philosophizing that goes on in the poems from late 1922 until the end of 1925 is of a special sort, and is in a paradoxical way consistent with the genial hostility to reason Graves expressed in the poems through the first half of *Whipperginney*. Though he now reasons, he does not believe in reason any more than he did in 1916 or will in 1966. The thinking mind only knows that it does not know what it knows, and that language cannot express what the mind knows it does not know. Graves, having looked within, now looked around, and found that there was nothing to see, except what the spectator thought he saw. So,

> With no sure knowledge but that knowledge changes
> Beyond all local proof or local disproof,   (*Marmosite, 5*)

he ruminates on

> The colour of pure thought
> The texture of emptiness,   (*Hose, 36*)

sure that

> Since knowledge is but folly's spy
> It is not sane to know.   (*Beggar, 77*)

These poems are about "remembered conflicts of an earlier heat" (*Whipperginney*, 43). He considers problems, questions, uncertainties, contentions, arguments, antinomies, imperfections; hesitantly offers hypotheses, theses, syntheses, and counterarguments; but ends up with incertitudes, irreconcilabilities, contrarieties, "thought amazements," conundrums, equivocations, paradoxes, riddles, "verbal quags," and new cause for dispute; he poses idealists against materialists, nuns against

[17]

agnostics, priests against atheists, dialecticians against dullards, colonialists against colonials; he shows us

> creeds, religions, nations
> Combatant together
> With mutual damnations
>
> (*Whipperginney*, 29)

and decides that "wherever there is conflict, all sides are wrong" (*Marmosite*, 12). In any case, "I dislike them all impartially" (*Beggar*, 31),

> One sort of error
> Being no worse than any other.   (*Hose*, 2)

Once you have seen "The gardens of the mind fall waste" (*Hose*, 49), once you know that "thought has a bias" (*Whipperginney*, 16), you are not inclined to take sides in epistemological disputes: "What is Mind? No Matter. What is matter? Never mind" (*Marmosite*, 8). Nor will moral issues engage you: "Between good an devil I strive not to judge" (*Marmosite*, 12). Nor will theological ones, because

> if God is, he must be blind
> Or if he was, is dead.   (*Owl*, 59)

You will perhaps keep busy by trying to state the issue, if there is one; you will ask yourself

> how am I to put
> The question that I'm asking you to answer?
>
> (*Hose*, 38)

or you will distract yourself with trivia and laugh at yourself for asking what is not only unanswerable but unaskable; or you will seek other consolations:

> Contentious weary,
>   It giddies all to think;
> Then kiss, girl, kiss!
>   Or drink, fellow, drink!
>
> (*Whipperginney*, 16)

[18]

You will neither take sides nor let your emotions be aroused, and if others find your non-position untenable, let them:

> Do you, my cribbed empiricist
> Judge these things false, then false they'll be.
>
> *(Beggar, 23)*

In any case, Graves continues, he was only doing what he had no choice but to do: "He had no option: as he did, he did" (*Beggar*, 32). The philosophizing in these poems is what fairyland is in the earlier volumes, a form of escape. As fairyland in the earlier poems took his mind off the war, so philosophizing in the poems from 1922 to 1925 took his mind off his mind, which had been disordered by the war. And Graves knows all this himself. Doubt is self-protective, he explains in "Antinomies"; to take one side is to leave oneself open to revenge from the other. Equivocation is a way of holding oneself together.

In "These oafish works of my outlandish hand" (*Beggar*, 3), then, these poems of "bland depreciation" (*Hose*, 45), of "mirth-abstracted joy,/ Calm terror, noiseless rage" (*Whipperginney*, 1), we see the fruits of Graves's new discovery that "the poet is no genie armed with fire" (*Hose*, 46). On these "cold shores of philosophic musing" (*Beggar*, 3), we are told, "Joy and passion both are spent" (*Whipperginney*, 3). And by and large the weary wit and the musings on philosophical paradox seem to have put out the fire in his head. But there was smoke. One type of poem, recurrent through this period, lets us see what the abstractions and the wit are hiding, and the poems of this type are very nearly the only poems of this period to have survived into Graves's recent collections.

In the mood of *On English Poetry* he had written a poem called "The Rock Below" (*Whipperginney*, 40–41). In it the narrator hears the earth telling him to pull up a clump of weeds

[19]

—"Search what hides below." He does so and finds "Stumps of thorn with ancient crooks." He wrenches these loose and plants a rosebush in their place. For a while the rosebush gives him pleasure, but then it begins to cry out that its roots are strangling on a rock below. In a rage he pulls out the bush and begins striking the rock. Despair overtakes him. He wonders if roses will ever again flower for him and if "heart and back" are too slightly built for the strain of pulling the rock out. He screws up his courage—"steely fingers hook in the crack"—tugs, and out comes peace of mind and poetry in the form of a "phoenix-tree" bearing "fruits of immortality." The moral of this Riversan parable is that if at first you don't succeed in rooting out whatever it is that ruins your health and strangles your poetic impulses, take courage, be persistent in your quest for self-knowledge: relief and poetry will follow.

But by 1924, when he published *The Meaning of Dreams*, and probably sooner, Graves had made an unsettling discovery: the attempt to root out one's neurosis by tracking down dream-symbols is self-defeating: "The deeper we burrow into our own minds, the farther these symbols retreat, becoming no longer well-known symbols, or even symbols of such symbols, but symbols of symbols of symbols. The attempt to overtake such knowledge is like chasing one's shadow from street lamp to street lamp. The further from the lamp behind the longer the shadow grows, the nearer to the next lamp the fainter it grows." The best poems of the period 1922–25 dramatize this discovery and related ones. In "Unicorn and White Doe" (*Whipperginney*, 8–10), the unicorn, after twenty thousand years' sleep, pursues the white doe. But "with briar/ And mire the tangled alleys crook/ Baulking desire." For all of his speed and his heart-bursting effort the unicorn never gets more of her than a glint of white or a shaking bough, never gets closer than within earshot of her taunting song, to which he responds:

[20]

I pursue, you fade
I run, you hide from me
In the glade.

The landscape of "Red Ribbon Dream" (*Whipperginney*, 27–28) is more specifically mental. A man stands "by a stair-head in the upper hall." The doors around him are locked "as before." As the scenery shifts and dissolves around him, he stands "quite dumb, sunk fast in the mire." But a voice says "come" and he follows "with no thought or doubt." He is led to a land of the heart's desire, presided over by a beauty he recognizes as his "fate and all" by the thin red ribbon on her calm brow. "Then I was a hero and a bold boy"; but as he kisses her, the ribbon twists in his own hair. There is a sudden break. The poem and the bold boy end as they began:

I stand by the stair-head in the upper hall;
The rooms to the left and right are locked as before.

The Feather Bed (1923) is a long poem narrated by a neurotic. "It is a study of a fatigued mind in a fatigued body and under the stress of an abnormal conflict," Graves explains in the introduction. He later suppressed the body of the poem, the epilogue, and part of the prologue. In the part he did not suppress (renamed "The Witches' Cauldron" in later collections) a man wanders in mist that "Confused the compass of the traveller's mind,/ Biased his course," limping, stumbling down and down through a dream landscape of "falls of scree, moss-mantled slippery rocks/ Wet bracken, drunken gurgling water-courses," over marshes and ridges, but always comes back to the same place:

The same sedged pool of steaming desolation
The same black monolith rearing up before it.

The theme of getting nowhere, especially of getting nowhere by trying to find the way in that is the only way out, continued to inform the poetry of the next phase of Graves's career, the phase of reconstruction, 1920 through 1929. Three excellent poems from that period, for example, "The Castle," "The Cool Web," "Warning to Children," deal with one or another form of this theme. But during the thirties this discouraging subject gradually disappeared; Graves then knew where he was going —toward the Goddess. In "The Cell" (later called "The Philosopher"), a poem written sometime between 1930 and 1933, the trapped mind, "Ruling out memory and fantasy" as well as the distractions of the body, finds "solace" in building "a spacious other head"

> In which the emancipated reason might
> Learn in due time to walk at greater length
> And more answerably.

By 1944 Graves had constructed the White Goddess myth, that solacing and spacious other head, wholly emancipated from reason; this myth is at once the rock below, the land of his heart's desire, presided over by a red-ribbon girl, full of white does and witches' cauldrons. Graves was in where he both wanted and had to be, and no longer worried about not being able to find the way out.

Graves found his way between 1925 and the turn of the decade. He became then the kind of man he still is, and his poems became pretty much what they still are, in form and intention, if not in subject. *Poems, 1926–1930* is the first volume of the authentic and unique Graves. A number of outside influences, conspiring with his own inner development, brought the transformation about.

In the middle of 1925 Graves found substitutes for Basanta Mallik, an Indian philosopher, and T. E. Lawrence, the man of ideas as a man of action, who had been the main influences behind the philosophizing poems of 1922–25 and the philosophizing *Poetic Unreason* (1925), Graves's second book of

[22]

criticism. Mallik was much concerned with the relativity of all things, notably values, but he also insisted on "strict self-discipline" and "constant self-watchfulness against either dominating or being dominated by any other individual." Lawrence's great theme was the illusory nature of all things. The works of men, Lawrence told Graves, are "all parts of an illusion, like ourselves, and our ideas, and our knowledge, and our universe."

Graves's next critical books, *Contemporary Techniques of Poetry; a Political Analogy* (1925), *Another Future of Poetry* (1926), and *A Survey of Modernist Poetry* (1927), reflect different influences. These books trace both Graves's increasing lack of sympathy for the times and his increasing sympathy for the aims and practices of the new poets, especially Frost, Ransom, and Cummings, whom Graves met, liked, and helped get published in England. But the main cause of this momentary flirtation with modernism was another American, Laura Riding, with whom Graves was to remain in close association for thirteen years. "In 1925 I first became acquainted with the poems and critical work of Laura Riding, and in 1926 with herself; and slowly began to revise my whole attitude toward poetry."

Louise Cowan, the historian of the American Fugitive poets, describes Riding as having a "nominal relationship" with that group. Those courtly southern gentlemen offered to take her under their wings, but soon found themselves faced with the threat of being forced to become her disciples. "Always you get the impression that the Devil and all Pandemonium couldn't dissuade her of her tendency," said Allen Tate. There was "some little discussion," and the poetess in search of a disciple left for England, where she found what she was looking for. In the "Dedicatory Epilogue" to his autobiography Graves reminds her how, on her arrival, "there was thereupon a unity to which you and I pledged our faith and she [Graves's wife] her pleasure."

Her surprising, and to Robert Graves good, news was that "historic Time had effectively come to an end." "All the historical events have happened," she noted. The poet who tries to express the spirit of the times, then, can only write "poetry of an obituary nature." The true poet is concerned with "the single event possible after everything has happened: a determination of values." Poetry determines values not by distributing praise or blame but by uncovering truth, "truth as a compound of completeness and order—a universe of values," with reference to which the historical events that no longer occur can be judged. Life cannot judge poetry, because the latter "is its own world, and to be corroborated by its own test of reality." Its truth is not logical, but "supra-logical," to use Graves's term, and challenges "the spatio-temporal structure which the civilized intellect has built for its habitation."

The poem is not the poet's creation but his discovery. "Poetry invents itself." It is "a selfness," but not of the poet. His function is to help bring to maturity "something of which some slight clue has been given." He can only perform this function if he is only himself, or he will confuse poetry's selfness with his own. So though his method is to use "words in poetry with the true voice and the true mind of oneself," he does not express his personal self, as Graves used to think—he expresses a transpersonal truth, but one that his self-discipline enables him alone to perceive. As the poetic universe is critical of any other, such as the universe of facts, by being only itself —truth—so the poet is a critic of his time by trying to preserve himself from it, by trying to be only himself: "The structure of the poetic universe is directed by a person in singlehanded conflict with the time-community."

These heady ideas have remained a part of Graves's intellectual equipment ever since. *The White Goddess*, for example, is an attempt to relate the themes, myths, characters, and scenery of this poetic universe, and is, by its very nature, an adverse judgment of the time-community. Graves was so willing to take over Riding's ideas because she only told him what he had all along wanted to say, but had been unable to find the words for in his skeptical terminology of 1922–25. She showed him how to recover value without submitting to group value, and how to recover his faith in poetry without compromising his skepticism about anything else. Unlike his other reality-instructors, Riding made him more rather than less himself. In Graves's words, she "No monster made but me."

While Riding was making him over into himself he was helping her along by writing those attempts at self-definition through extrication that the poetry and prose of 1926–30 are. In the prose, especially, he tried to shake off all the involvements, historical, national, social, literary, intellectual, domestic, and emotional, that had stopped him from being only his own, and Laura Riding's, man. In the poetry there is equal emphasis on the converse process of integration, on defining what was being uncovered by the process of extrication. The culmination of this latter process and its greatest monument is Graves's prose masterpiece, his autobiography, in which he described all that had made him what he was, only to say goodbye to it. Writing the last page on his thirty-fourth birthday, he notes: "Another month of final revision and I shall have parted with myself for good."

But these processes can also be studied in the critical works Graves wrote either under Riding's influence or in collaboration with her. *Impenetrability; or, The Proper Habit of English* (1926); *Lars Porsena; or, The Future of Swearing and Improper Language* (1927); *A Survey of Modernist Poetry* (1927); *Mrs. Fisher; or, The Future of Humor* (1928); *Pamphlet Against Anthologies* (1928) are all both attacks on "the whole perfectly utterly goddawful raving world" and defenses of poetry (of which the "proper" use of English prose, swearing, and jokes are subspecies) as Laura Riding, and now Graves, understood it.

The main source of Graves's disaffection from nearly everything was "a complicated domestic crisis." In the first place, he was hard-pressed for money. His poems, which had enjoyed a vogue while their author was considered a war-poet, were no longer selling. He opened a grocery store only to mismanage it into bankruptcy. His attempt to earn a living as a professor at the newly founded Royal Egyptian University was turned into a fiasco by student riots, domestic troubles, and his own intractability. In May, 1929, Nancy Nicholson left him for good. In April, Laura Riding had come close to doing the same: she nearly died from a fall out of a fourth-story window. And around this same time, says Graves, he had "broken a good many conventions; quarrelled with, or been disowned by most of my friends; been grilled by the police on a suspicion of attempted murder; and ceased to care what anyone thought of me."

During the last years of the twenties, then, Graves was engaged in "a close and energetic study of the disgusting, the contemptible and the evil," especialy to the extent that he was involved in them, so that he could get them behind him forever. He finally cut loose in a very frenzy of exorcism in a play—all the more outrageous for being a play, the most public of literary forms—written immediately upon his arrival in Majorca, apparently, and included in a collection of addenda to his autobiography. Play and collection are both entitled *But It Still Goes On* (1930). In the play, "a tactful reshuffling of actual events and situations in which I had been more or less closely concerned," David, a homosexual, marries Dorothy, sister to Dick, whom David loves; and Charlotte, a lesbian, would have married Dick because she loves Dorothy, but out of an objectless spite marries Cecil, Dick's and Dorothy's father, who is nevertheless a rival of Dick's for Elizabetta, who is having an affair with Pritchard, who is a poet, as are his rivals, Dick and Cecil. Dorothy, learning of David's preference for men, shoots him. Charlotte, still spiteful, but now pregnant as well, claiming (dishonestly) that Dick has seduced her, maliciously commits suicide by throwing herself over a banister. Once the two queers are out of the way, the others, led by Dick, torment Cecil, representative of a vestigially prestigious older generation, into shooting himself. Remorseless over his dead body, they tell the police that he had confessed to murdering David. "When I fight I fight dirty," says Dick.

The sexual disorder, of course, is to be taken as symptomatic of a condition of society and a stage in history. Dick, Graves's spokesman, makes clear in word and deed

that the bottom of things, after working looser and looser for centuries, has at last fallen out; and that no public recognition has been made of what is after all the most important human catastrophe that's ever happened. I don't mean catastrophe in any tragic sense. Tragedy and comedy both fell through the hole. So did optimism and pessimism. And rebellion and reaction.

And honor and loyalty. And restraint and decency. And respect and pride. And responsibility and blame. And so on and so on. But the ultimate horror for these characters is "that it's finished and ended and over, but it still goes on," even though, as far as Graves was concerned, it was just plain finished. In the 1957 revision of his autobiography, Graves tells us that, although he has often been asked to publish a continuation of the story he had taken up to 1929, "I am always glad to report that little of outstanding autobiographical interest has happened since."

He exaggerates, of course, although one could not tell it from a reading of the poems Graves wrote from 1926 to 1944. *Poems,*

1926–1930, Poems, 1930–1933, Collected Poems, 1938, and *Poems 1938–1945* are personal without being confessional, exfoliations from experiences into new ones, rather than expositions of something Graves has in fact experienced. Each of the poems in these collections strives to be a separate and unique metaphor, closed off by the curve of its interlocking associations, for something Graves now understands that he had to accept or reject, fear or desire, perform or suffer, be or not be, rather than a literal narrative, raw exclamation, querulous gripe, or surly wrangle. Whereas in the earlier "fantastic" poems Graves's method was to place himself as subject in relation to some dream of gratified desire or to some nightmare of frustration and menace, his method is now to place himself, from poem to poem, as a series of personae—his "sub-personalities"—reacting to a variety of fully dramatized scenes. His poems have become in tendency now, as we say, ironic, objective, impersonal, dramatic; they have become, that is, poems.

With the new voices and new scenes come new forms and techniques, tones and moods, rhythms and images. For the old thumping ballads, jiggling Skeltonics, chummy verse letters, blank-verse antithesizing, and arch Mother Goosery, we now find a truly wonderful display of new forms, some of them unique modifications of traditional forms, such as the ballad, rhyme royal, the Sapphic, and late Jacobean blank verse, but others simply unique, even among Graves's work. "It Was All Very Tidy," for example, is a seven-stanza poem, each one of which ends with the words of the title. The first stanza contains seven lines, the second contains six, the third five, and so on until the seventh and last stanza, which contains nine: the single line we expect it to have, six others to sum up the other stanzas, a line to express the poet's wry acceptance of the situation—"He [Death] was not unwelcome"—and the refrain "It was all very tidy," as, indeed, it is. The equally ingenious

"Language of the Seasons" is another poem that illustrates what it discusses in the process of discussing it, only in this case it is imagery that does the job.

And when Graves does use one of his old forms he tends to do so with ironic self-consciousness, in such a way that the form becomes a comment, usually adverse, upon itself or upon the sentiment. In "Despite and Still," for example, the mere semantics of the poem presents a lover trying to convince his beloved that they should hold fast to their love despite the impediments that necessarily attend it, but the short, exactly rhyming, often run-on, Skeltonic lines qualify the sentiment with a jaunty irony; the form seems to say, "In spite of what I say, we both know it can't be done." In the sardonic "Lift-Boy," the nursery-rhyme form works against the matter to become an exposure of all the cautionary or improving sentiments to which children are exposed. In a similar vein, Graves will sometimes turn a genre, instead of a form, inside-out. "Landscapes," for example, is a nature poem, a utilization of the pathetic fallacy to attack not only nature poetry but Nature,

> Whose pleasures are excreting, poking,
> Havocking and sucking,
> Sleepy licking.
> Whose griefs are melancholy,
> Whose flowers are oafish,
> Whose waters, silly,
> Whose birds, raffish,
> Whose fish, fish.

The equally rude "Pavement" looks at first like a genre-scene of the picturesque Wm. Brazier, chimney sweep, with his pretty horse, Scot, and his cheery greetings to children, "Hello, my dears!" But two bracketed passages show us what the Wm. Braziers are really like and how their greetings really sound, "Scum off, you damn young milliner's bastards you!" Here's the way the poem ends:

> [. . . Let them copy it out on a pink page of their albums,
> Carefully leaving out the bracketed lines
> It's an old story—f's for s's—
> But good enough for them, the suckers.]

The use of rhyme and metre is equally self-conscious. Instead of a regular progress of exact rhymes filling out a series of formally alike stanzas, we get irregular rhyme, the rhyming of weak and strong syllables, consonance, dissonance, and even the absence of rhyme, in each case sounding against a background of every possible kind of metrical variation, including substitutions in the delicate second and forth feet of iambic pentameter, and including additions to or subtractions from the expected number of feet. Sometimes Graves will pit a single turbulent rhythm, extending from the first word to the last, against the stanzaic metrical divisions. Or he will interrupt the declarative flow with a question or aside, or even more characteristically, avoid any resolution whatsoever by ending a poem with a final ambiguous question. But a thwarting or mockery of the reader's expectations by avoidances of resolution, by anticlimax, or by melopoetic surprise is a characteristic tendency of this period. The paradigm of this tendency is "Leaving the Rest Unsaid," which ends like this:

> Therefore, my solemn ones, leaving the rest unsaid,
> Rising in air, as on a cherub's wings,
> At a careless comma,

Many of these technical surprises function specifically and locally, as in, for example, Eliot's famous *ices-crises* rhyme, but their usual function is to give the poem a general rough, aggressive, insistently individual quality, and to express Graves's rejection of his old self, the poetry being written around him, and the reader's predilections. These last are rejected directly, as well as formally, in "Boy of Naples," where the reader is described as

[30]

> The blind man reading Dante upside-down
> And not in Braille. . . .

In "To the Reader over My Shoulder" Graves tells the titular hero to leave off playing

> creaking grind-stone to my wit.
> Know me, have done: I am a clean spirit
> And you, for ever flesh.   Have done.

"Know me, have done" might be a motto over the poems written from 1926 to 1944, for that, in poem after poem, is what Graves says to himself. He sets out to know himself, so that he can have done with the rest. In the process of self-definition he tries to distinguish what is peculiarly his own from what is the common human fate and from what is "local," the product of historical or social circumstance. That done, he is able to decide what can be discarded, what he should embrace, and what must be endured because there is no alternative. Unlike the earlier poems, then, which were "digressive" or evasive, these are poems of confrontation in behalf of self-definition and extrication.

In the least interesting of the poems of extrication, Graves simply confronts something, such as science or modern housing, to discover that it is not for him. In others, the attitude is something like, "That was part of me, take it or leave it," to: "That is me, and there's nothing I can do about it," to: "That is us, and there's nothing we can do about it." In a few conciliatory poems near the end of this period the attitude is something like, "That is not for me, it's of the past, but there may be something in it, I may have been wrong." (See "The Advocates," "A Country Mansion," "The Ages of Oath," "End of Play," "Midway," "Recalling War," "No More Ghosts," which are among the best poems of this period.) The cumulative tenor of the two dozen or so love poems is that love made him whatever he is that he can embrace without regret or resentment. But the complementary, and far more powerful, poems on lust, "Ulysses," "Down, Wanton, Down," "Succubus," "Leda," "The Beast," "A Jealous Man," and "Parent to Children," are of the "That is us, and there is nothing we can do about it" variety. They make the love poems seem frail by comparison.

By the end of this period, to anticipate, Graves, having distinguished the desirable from the necessary in himself and having extricated these from the rest, is able to contemplate his own poetic image as that of a man with whom he could live. And he did so with a certain complacency, in the way of self-made men. The next step was to create a world in which that man could feel at home, and in 1944, with the invention of the White Goddess, he took that step. Like many another man, Graves came to feel that it was not enough to believe in oneself alone, but again, like other men, he found it easiest to believe in a "spacious other head," in his own psyche mythologized. The struggle to bring himself into being, however, during the eighteen years preceding the Goddess, produced in my opinion more good poems than the subsequent poetry of self-transcendence.

The acceptance or admission of limitation, the refusal to be ambitious or to expect too much either from oneself or from things in general, is the great theme of the poems of self-definition. In poem after poem Graves tries to purge himself of beguiling illusions, great expectations, and self-indulgent terrors. See, for example, "Hector," "Philatelist Royal," and "The Cool Web," poems about the limitations of poetry itself; "Lost Acres" and "In No Directions," poems about the impossibility of complete knowledge and the contingent nature of human choices; "The Suicide in the Copse," "The Halls of Bedlam," "The Shot," and "The Rock on the Corner," poems rejecting the interesting malaise and despair that lead to suicide and madness.

The self finally defined is one free to go its own awkward, stiff, crooked, slow, bumbling, unambitious, unhoodwinkable, incorruptible, wayward way. The stammering, awkward hero of "Gardener" for example, has, in spite of crooked rows and ill-pruned boughs, the loveliest flowers, the most glorious fruit. He attributes his success to a guardian angel; he has, in fact,

> An ass's wit, a hairy-belly shrewdness
> That would appraise the intentions of the angel
> By the very distance of his own confusion
> And bring the most to pass.

"Ordinary," except to the extent that he is "wayward" (two of his favorite words during this period), Graves will banish the uncanny by a devotion to the commonplace tasks at hand and to poetry appropriate for dealing with them. In "Lollocks," to take one instance, the creatures of the title are malicious goblins "By sloth on sorrow fathered":

> Sovereign against Lollocks
> Are hard broom and soft broom,
> To well comb the hair,
> To well brush the shoe,
> And to pay every debt
> So soon as its due.

The spooks have been groomed out, we learn from "No More Ghosts," but they have left a shrunken world. Though the poet can finally exclaim, Look we have come through! and tell himself to "Have no more crowns of hope, and none of regret," the struggle has too richly rewarded him with poems and drama for him not to regret a little his victory over the vain longings and terrors and the illusory obligations he had left by the way. Having at first overextended himself, Graves, in this middle period, resolved not to let his reach exceed his grasp. He would practice integrity by keeping his hands in his pockets. While he was at it he started to act upon another notion he had about how to keep poetic faith: "I should say that my health as a poet lies in my mistrust of a comfortable point of rest." The outcome was that he once again became an overreacher; and while involving himself in illusory obligations to the Goddess he brought back all the self-indulgent terrors and vain longings.

Before turning to the Goddess, I should say a word about Graves's fiction, the best of which was written during the period of extrication and self-definition. The first of his sixteen novels is *My Head! My Head!* (1925) and the last is *They Hanged My Saintly Billy* (1957); these are Graves's worst. The best are *I, Claudius* (1934), *Claudius the God* (1935), *Count Belisarius* (1937), *The Golden Fleece* (1944; American title: *Hercules, My Shipmate*), and *King Jesus* (1946). Best and worst, Graves's novels, with only two exceptions, are historical novels. *Antigua, Penny, Puce* (1936; American title: *The Antigua Stamp*) and *No Decency Left* (1932; written with Laura Riding and published under the pseudonym "Barbara Rich") are satires of modern life in the mood of that low-minded play, *But It Still Goes On.* The rest range in setting from the legendary past of Moses in *My Head! My Head!* and of Hercules in *The Golden Fleece* to the future in *Seven Days in New Crete* (1949; American title: *Watch the Northwind Rise*).

But even in the historical novels most of the characters are like those in *But It Still Goes On.* Usually a good-hearted but simple-minded hero is undone by an environment of treachery, ambition, intrigue, and lust, at the center of which is a woman driven by all of these to an extreme degree. Examples of such heroes are Pedro Fernandez, in *Isles of Unwisdom* (1944), William Palmer, in *Saintly Billy*, Claudius, Belisarius, Benedict Arnold, and Judas Iscariot. But in *Story of Marie Powell, Wife to Mr. Milton* (1943), the good-hearted Marie is undone by the treacherous, ambitious, intriguing, and lustful womanly man,

[34]

John Milton. Working against the modern psychology (as Graves understands it) of the characters are loving and detailed descriptions of past rites, feasts, occupations, military strategy, dress, housing, and games. While the characters are usually flat and conventional types, such as the tricky slave, the bragging captain, the sly eunuch, the outspoken nurse, the resourceful companion, the popular and loyal general who is driven to rebellion or death by his jealous and tyrannical king, the bitchy beauty, and so on, the physical settings are always full, rich, strange, at once unique and convincing in their historicity. The contrast between the characters and the settings in which they move implies that people act and think with the same low-minded contemporaneity, no matter where or when they live.

That implication is not surprising in theory, but it makes for a continuous series of little aesthetic thrills, of minute recognitions of contemporary relevance amidst the historically remote, that is one of the major pleasures of Graves's fiction, and, incidentally, of his historical studies. The other major pleasure is produced by the contrast, derived from conventional history and common sense, of how we think things must have been and how the hidden conspiracies of Graves's characters make them look. We begin, for example, with some notion of what kind of emperor Claudius was, of what the American Revolution was like, of what Jesus and Milton were trying to do. But then we find in the Claudius novels that this "idealistic enemy of Caesardom" is made emperor against his will. So he does his best to bring Caesardom into disrepute by playing the fool. When the demoralized Romans stand for every one of his antics, no matter how outrageous, he becomes bitter, starts to out-Caligula Caligula, and chooses as his successor Nero, "whom he knew to be mad, egotistical and degenerate," in the hopes that all this would be enough to bring back the republic. "It nearly was."

Graves's Christ, in *King Jesus*, to take another example, is the son of Miriam of the House of David and of Antipater, son of Herod the Great. His genealogy, place and time of birth, character, and actions satisfy the prerequisites of the five different messiahs predicted by the prophets and awaited by the various Jewish sects. He becomes King of the Jews by marrying Mary, the real heir to the throne, but he refuses to consummate the marriage physically. His mission was, he thinks, to end worship of the mother goddess—"I have come to destroy the work of the female"—and to reform morals according to Pharisaic doctrine as interpreted by Hillel. But he fails. "His fault was this: that he tried to force the hour of doom by declaring war on the female. But the female abides." After his resurrection, which is euhemeristically explained, Christ goes off into a twenty-year exile in Rome, and his teachings are perverted by Paul.

Similarly, *Homer's Daughter* shows us the *Odyssey* written by a sixth-century Sicilian girl; in *Story of Marie Powell* Milton writes his divorce tracts out of frustrated hair-fetishism; *Sergeant Lamb's America* (1940) and *Proceed, Sergeant Lamb* (1941) show us American Revolutionaries commanded by jealous opportunists, inspired by rabble-rousers universally married to lecherous women, losing every battle but winning the war through the misfortune and generosity of the British, putting on a poor show at the Battle of Bunker Hill, which is fought somewhere else, and executing their most capable and loyal general, Benedict Arnold. We only provisionally accept or tolerate this nonsense because of the fullness and factuality of the settings; because every event we think of as established historical fact is accounted for; because it makes us feel superior to assume with Graves that people do things only out of the worst but most easily intelligible motives; because we take it as fiction written for fictional purposes.

But the distinction between fiction and history is not a clear one to Graves, for temperamental as well as theoretical reasons.

In the introduction to a recent (1964) collection of stories, after telling us that most of the stories "are true," he goes on to say that he cannot "claim to have invented the factual details" of even the most bizarre pieces, and concludes: "Pure fiction is beyond my imaginative range." So, we might add, is pure fact. If, as Graves said in 1949, he earns his income "by writing history disguised as novels," he supplements that income by writing fiction disguised as history. And he writes both by the same method—"the analeptic method—the intuitive recovery of forgotten events by a deliberate suspension of time."

More concretely, as Graves explained in *Poetic Unreason*, the historian, or scholar, or critic, like the novelist, saturates himself in the details of whatever he is investigating until his mind selects as salient whatever answers to his emotional or intellectual needs. These selected details arrange themselves in configurations according to the associative habits of the mind that selects. Once the resulting structure is expressed in words, it becomes a metaphor of that mind. The mind provides shape, motive, and continuity according to its own laws. In the finished product, the construct, the observer, and the observed are one. The apologetic introduction to Graves's first novel denies "that the thing known and the thinker can co-exist with the thought, and that the thing known has a merely passive part to play. With me it is an article of belief that the thinker is also the thing known, and the thing known also the thinker; and that when the thought comes, both the thing known and the thinker, as such, must disappear."

And that is why *King Jesus* (a novel) and both *Jesus in Rome* (1957) and *The Nazarene Gospel Restored* (1954) (works of historical exposition); *My Head! My Head!* (a novel about Moses) and both *Adam's Rib* (1955) and *The Hebrew Myths* (1963) (works constructing the "original" Old Testament); *Homer's Daughter* (a novel) and the sections on the Homeric

[37]

epics in *The Greek Myths* (1955) as well as the *Anger of Achilles* (1959) (a version of the *Iliad*); both *Watch the Northwind Rise* (a novel about a future ruled by the White Goddess) and *Hercules, My Shipmate* (a novel about a legendary past ruled by the Goddess) and *The White Goddess*—why all of these are written in the same playful spirit and with equal amounts of history and fiction, as these are usually understood, and good amounts of autobiography.

It follows that the angry splutters of scholars—"It is about time that someone protested Graves's misuse of his great imaginative gifts in muddying every scholarly water he touches," says Stanley Edgar Hyman—are largely irrelevant. Irrelevant to us, that is; Graves takes such splutters seriously. He once demanded a public apology from a man who wrote that *The Nazarene Gospel Restored* was the work of "a renegade Protestant." Graves is serious about his scholarship as a man is serious about his life, even if he is by profession a player. The imaginative gift and the muddy waters are one.

While engaged in research for *Hercules, My Shipmate*, Graves was interrupted by "a sudden overwhelming obsession." He was overtaken by a vision of "the pre-Aryan Triple Moon-Goddess—sometimes called Leucothea, the White Goddess," and by a sudden insight into the meanings of a truly astounding number of rites, ancient beliefs, myths, icons, magical practices, natural and cosmic symbols, forgotten campaigns, and memorable ecstasies. "I seem to have stumbled on the central secret of neolithic and Bronze Age religious faith."

Whether the interruption was sudden or not, it had been for a long time preparing itself: W. H. R. Rivers, whose influence on Graves was immense, had been much interested in Melanesian magic and mother goddesses. Sir James Frazer and his Cambridge followers, whom Graves was reading during the twenties, were interested in similar things. And the romantic English poetry that held Graves in thrall up to the mid-twenties was rich in fatal women and mana-ridden landscapes. The important women in Graves's life were of a matriarchal bent as well. Though his father was a poet, Graves always remembers "how much more I owe, as a writer, to my mother than to my father." "There was a man once, a Frenchman," she used to say, "who died of grief because he could not become a mother." Nancy Nicholson was an uncompromising feminist, but like Athena "all-for-the-male" compared to Laura Riding, who flatly declared that woman "is the answer to the question 'Does God exist?'" The story goes that written in large gold letters on her bedroom wall in Majorca was the legend GOD IS A WOMAN.

And how could Graves disagree? He knew the very woman in whom God was incarnate. The last poem in *Poems, 1930–1933* addresses Laura Riding as Isis-Hecate-Lilith. In "To the Sovereign Muse," a poem-sequence published in 1935, Laura Riding is the Goddess as Muse, and the poet is her king, "vanquished of the moon." Was the Goddess Laura Riding, then? In a way:

> Which was the Goddess, which the woman?
> Let the philosophers break their teeth on it!

> (*New Poems, 1962*, 23)

Does the Goddess really exist? Graves equivocates again: "Whether God is a metaphor or a fact cannot be reasonably argued: let us likewise be discreet on the subject of the Goddess."

Although Graves addresses the Goddess as "You, most unmetaphorically you," it is clear that the Goddess system is one of those unified structures of correspondences, of interlocking motifs, images, and metaphors, such as medieval and renaissance poets were supposed to have had in the Great Chain of Being.

[39]

But no poet since Milton, and perhaps not Milton, seems to have been able to accept that impossible mélange of Plato's *Timaeus*, Thomistic theology, hierarchies derived from the Pseudo-Dionysius, and suchlike. A number of modern poets have found it necessary to do for themselves what Blake had already done for himself and what earlier poets had not to do. *The White Goddess* (1948), like Yeats's *A Vision*, Auden's *The Enchafèd Flood*, and Lawrence's *Fantasia of the Unconscious*, is a storehouse of metaphors for poetry, an ideal world of archetypal images in which each item is resonant with overtones of meaning sounded by all the other items, to which it has hierarchical or analogical relationships.

The Goddess system, then, is that "spacious other head" we noticed Graves looking for earlier, a world more attractive than the modern one he by 1929 had left behind him, or to one side. "I must Create a System or be enslav'd by another Man's," said Blake, and Graves would agree. Graves's system is a *paysage moralisé*, rather than a landscape from which nymphs and value have departed. And as such, it is one from which he can judge "all that." But as the landscape of his mind given a habitation and a name, the world of the Goddess is at once distanced from Graves and only his own. He can roam through it as a man of property, or as an explorer, or as a culture hero calling things into existence by giving them names. He can therefore be impersonal about his own image, be cold and passionate at once.

The White Goddess, as the subtitle tells us, is a "Historical Grammar of Poetic Myth," an exposition of the language out of which all true poems are made. Only gold can be turned into gold, says Graves, thinking of the modernist poetic alchemists, and "only poetry into poems." For the true poet there is one story and one story only, and it has only one theme; all the rest is verse, and leaden verse at that:

The theme, briefly, is the antique story, which falls into thirteen chapters and an epilogue, of the birth, life, death, and resurrection of the God of the Waxing Year; the central chapters contain the God's losing battle with the God of the Waning Year for love of the capricious and all-powerful Threefold Goddess, their mother, bride, and layerout. The poet identifies himself with the God of the Waxing Year and his Muse with the Goddess; the rival is his blood-brother, his other self, his weird. All true poetry—true by Housman's practical test—celebrates some incident or scene in this very ancient story, and the three main characters are so much a part of our racial inheritance that they not only assert themselves in poetry but recur on occasions of emotional stress in the form of dreams, paranoiac visions, and delusions. The weird, or rival, often appears in nightmare as the tall, lean, dark-faced bed-side spectre, or Prince of the Air, who tries to drag the dreamer out through the window, so that he looks back and sees his body still lying rigid in bed, but he takes countless other malevolent or diabolic or serpent-like forms.

The Goddess is a lovely, slender woman with a hooked nose, deathly pale face, lips red as rowan berries, startlingly blue eyes and long fair hair; she will suddenly transform herself into sow, mare, bitch, vixen, she-ass, weasel, serpent, owl, she-wolf, tigress, mermaid or loathsome hag. Her names and titles are innumerable. In ghost stories she often figures as "The White Lady," and in ancient religions, from the British Isles to the Caucasus, as the "White Goddess." I cannot think of any true poet from Homer onwards who has not independently recorded his experience of her. The test of a poet's vision, one might say, is the accuracy of his portrayal of the White Goddess and of the island over which she rules. The reason why the hairs stand on end [Housman's test], the skin crawls and a shiver runs down the spine when one reads or writes a true poem is that a true poem is necessarily an invocation of the White Goddess, or Muse, the Mother of all Living, the ancient power of fright and lust—the female spider or the queen bee whose embrace is death.

Whereas the early outlandish poems were, in Graves's word, "digressive," the new ones, the Goddess poems, are regressive, in a number of ways, some of them easily unearthed by the depth psychology I have been studiously avoiding. Roam "through the heaped treasury of your heart:/ You will find her," Graves tells himself. Muse poems, if written by poets who have not read *The White Goddess,* are products of "an inspired, almost pathological reversion to the original language." They are "products of morbid psychology." Paying service to the Muse, in fact, is a way of attending to one's neurosis:

The pathology of poetic composition is no secret. A poet finds himself caught in some baffling emotional problem which is of such urgency that it sends him into a sort of trance. And in this trance his mind works, with astonishing boldness and precision, on several imaginative levels at once. The poem is either a practical answer to his problem, or else it is a clear statement of it; and a problem clearly stated is half-way to solution. Some poets are more plagued than others with emotional problems, and more conscientious in working out poems which arise from them—that is to say more attentive in their service to the Muse.

Through the Goddess Graves allowed himself to revert not only to his early romantic poetic subjects but also to his early theories as to how verse is written and why it makes one feel good to write it.

A number of the earlier poems in which Graves serves his Muse and tends to his neurosis, in *Poems, 1938–1945, Collected Poems, 1914–1947, Poems and Satires, 1951,* and *Poems, 1953,* are expository or programmatic, outlines and advertisements for the system. The best of these is "To Juan at the Winter Solstice," wherein we are told that "There is one story and one story only," which the poem then goes on to narrate. Others of these first Goddess poems, such as "The Allansford Pursuit," "The Alphabet Calendar of Amergin," "The Battle of the Trees," and "The Song of Blodeuwedd," are translations or restorations of ancient or renaissance charms, riddles, or narratives written in the only true poetic language. The first Goddess poem Graves wrote, and one of the "truly good" poems of modern literature—it is one of Graves's few rhythmical triumphs—"Instructions to the Orphic Adept," is in part a translation from the Egyptian Book of the Dead.

[42]

Most of the other early Goddess poems are ballad-like drama-
tizations of some episode or scene in the story of the hero-poet's
relations with the Muse. Graves's favorite scene, one that brings
to the fore "the pathology of poetic composition," depicts the
poet-sacred king-shaman-hero, trembling with fear and devotion, dazed, submissive, and awaiting his sacrificial dismemberment at the loving hands of the Goddess. He anticipates with
pleasure what he fears because he knows that his devotion will
be rewarded with immortality in an Apple Island paradise.
Dismemberment and Paradise combine to form Graves's favorite metaphor for requited love of the Goddess, who has her
ghoulish aspects:

> She has gnawn at corpse-flesh till her breath stank,
> Paired with a jackel, grown distraught and lank.
>
> (*Man Does, Woman Is*, 24)

And, as the poet reminds himself,

> Your true anguish
> Is all that she requires.   (*Poems, 1953*, 17)

He knows

> . . . I may not hope to dwell apart
> With you on Apple Island
> Unless my breast be docile to the dart,
>
> (*More Poems, 1961*, 10)

which it consequently, and often exasperatingly, is. Quivering
in romantic agonies of anticipation of the ultimate *frisson*—
being clawed and bitten to shreds by a beautiful and contemp-
tuous woman—does not sit well with the accompanying claims
of sturdy individualism, manly courage, and moral superiority,
although it is a combination we have come to accept from
various Victorian types.

For all that, a number of these poems have the elusive, haunt-
ing quality that makes "Thomas the Rimer," Blake's "Mental
Traveller," Keats's "La Belle Dame sans Merci," and Brown-

[43]

ing's "Childe Roland to the Dark Tower Came" the inexhaustibly suggestive poems they are. Let me recommend the following (from the volumes listed above), which in one way or another seem to make good Graves's claim about racial inheritances, standing hairs, and crawling skins: "Lament for Pasiphae," "The Destroyer," "The White Goddess," "The Young Cordwainer" (Graves's "Bavarian Gentians"), "Darien," and "Dethronement."

About one third of the new poems Graves published in the volumes from *Poems, 1938–1945* through *Poems, 1953* are Goddess poems. The others are of the kinds Graves was writing from 1926 to 1944, only less urgent and convincing, as though he had continued to write them out of habit. There are no new Goddess poems in *Collected Poems, 1955* and *Collected Poems, 1959*, although there are plenty of new poems. But a number of the love poems Graves wrote between 1944 and 1959, such as "The Portrait," "Your Private Way," "Woman and Tree," and "Forbidden Words," anticipate the kinds of Goddess poems Graves would write from 1960 to 1966, and these are almost the only kinds of poems he did write then.

In 1963 Graves explained that "only during the past three years have I ventured to dramatize truthfully and factually, the vicissitudes of a poet's dealings with the White Goddess, the perpetual Other Woman." These vicissitudes are described in *More Poems, 1961*, in *New Poems, 1962*, and in the first half of *Man Does, Woman Is* (1964). The second half of the last volume, Sections XVII and XVIII of *Collected Poems, 1965*, and the new poems in *Love Respelt* (1966) dramatize as well the poet's dealings with a new character, the Black Goddess, "his more-than-Muse." Graves's work between 1960 and 1966, then, has been to compose a one hundred seventy-five poem "sequence dramatizing the vicissitudes of poetic love."

The sequence is too long to be adequately summarized here, but I might give the reader a few guideposts to ease his own way through it. A good general introduction to these poems would be a book such as Maurice Valency's *In Praise of Love; an Introduction to the Love-Poetry of the Renaissance* (1958). The characters, situations, themes, and even the forms of troubadour and renaissance love poetry are pretty much those we find in Graves's sequence. Sometimes Graves's adherence to the courtly love conventions sets him in uncharacteristic postures, like this bit of Platonizing:

> Desire, first, by a natural miracle
> United bodies, united hearts, blazed beauty;
> Transcended bodies, transcended hearts.
> Two souls, now unalterably one
> In whole love always and forever,
> Soar out of twilight, through upper air,
> Let fall their sensuous burden.   (*Love Respelt*, 40)

Once again the knight claims that he and his lady are "twin paragons" of love, "love's exemplars." Once again he tells her "none alive shall view again/ The match of you and me." Once again the "dauntless" and lionhearted knight—"My name is Lion"—is made gentle and submissive by the lady, whose hair and eyes are as prominent and potent as ever. Once again his code of honor is to him what her beauty is to her—"Be beauty yours, be honor mine." Once again the only desirable love is adulterous love. The lady, Graves tells us in an essay, and demonstrates in the poems, agrees with the Countess of Narbonne: "Conjugal affection has absolutely nothing in common with love. We say 'absolutely,' and with all consideration, that love cannot exist between husband and wife." Once again the lady is both woman and Muse. To love her is to be inspired by her, and to be inspired by her is to write poems that are at once a record, a proof, and an analysis of that love. Once again, since,

[45]

in Graves's words, "the basis of poetry is love," to write love poems is to write about the writing of poems.

Once again the lovers' natural setting is "A moon-warmed world of discontinuance" more real "Than this pale outer world." They are "Sole woman and sole man," amidst "crowds of almost-men and almost-women," zombies, in fact, the "undead," who live in "the land of the dead." But the lady has granted her champion "power to stem/ The tide's unalterable flow."

> "Mistress," I cried, "the times are evil
> And you have charged me with their remedy,
>
> (*Poems and Satires, 1951*, 19)

and that is why "Others admire us as we walk this world."

The arrogance is extraordinary, though usual with Graves, but the theme is no less hoary than the others that inform this sequence. These poems are conventional rather than cliché-ridden, however. True, we hear too often, and sometimes bathetically, that love is a flame, that "To be near her is to be near the furnace." True, Graves develops a few tics of his own: seven of the first fifteen poems in *Man Does, Woman Is*, like many others, end in a question. True, the continuously repeated language of *promising*—oath, swear, forsworn, forsake, faith, debt, owe, pardon, vow, pledge, pact, and bond—begins to lose its sharpness. But a number of special features save the sequence from cliché.

Whereas the female character in renaissance love poetry was primarily a lady, secondarily endowed with attributes of the Muse, and only thirdly a recognizable woman, and further only lady, Muse, woman intermittently, Graves's female character is equally and simultaneously a fully characterized woman and a Muse, and her ladylike attributes of royalty, nobility, and aristocratic pride result from the interaction between her divinity and her very specific womanliness. There is always an am-

[46]

biguity, a bifocal quality about her, as in a double exposure with both exposures exceptionally clear. Even when she is falling in debt, sleeping out a hangover, or consorting with low-life there is a nimbus of divinity about her which will suddenly crystallize and brighten out her superimposed humanity, so that the latter shows as only a kind of delicate tracery. And with the divinity comes her environment, so that sun, tea party, kitsch, and gossip turn into moon, sacrificial dance, gold and malachite, and sirens' song.

Nor is the Goddess who possesses or "rides" the woman any pale remnant of classical mythology. The Goddess incarnate in a woman appears first as the difference between what a masculine pipe-dream of the woman would have her be and what that woman really is. She is as various as the ways in which a woman can confound or exceed masculine expectations. In Graves's verse she appears only seldom as Vesta, Goddess of the Hearth, faithful, innocent, old-fashioned, and companionate. Most often she appears as the White Goddess, proud, capricious, greedy, evasive, childish, murderous, unfaithful, lunatic, in love only with herself, demanding all and promising nothing. But in the last few years she has begun to appear as the Black Goddess, who

promises a new pacific bond between men and women, corresponding to a final reality of love, in which the patriarchal marriage bond will fade away. Unlike Vesta, the Black Goddess has experienced good and evil, love and hate, truth and falsehood in the person of her sister; but chooses what is good; rejecting serpent love and corpse flesh. Faithful as Vesta, gay and adventurous as the White Goddess, she will lead man back to that sure instinct of love which he long ago forfeited by intellectual pride.

A man who has found the Black Goddess has also found a comfortable resting point, one would think, but I doubt that Graves has. He spent the first ten years of his career, from 1916 to 1926, moving from conventional romanticism to conventional skepticism. For the next twenty years or so he brought his poetic self into being through poems of self-definition and extrication. For twenty years since then he has been celebrating his Muse. As I write these words, on his seventieth birthday, the evidence is that he is on his way to delighting and exasperating us for the next twenty years. The question is, how.

SELECTED BIBLIOGRAPHY

NOTE: *Graves's most important books are mentioned by title and date of first publication in the text. His English publisher is Cassell, his American, Doubleday. The student who wants to give Graves an extended look might consult F. H. Higginson:* A Bibliography of the Works of Robert Graves (*London, 1966*). *But for the general reader, who will no doubt want to start with samples of Graves's best work in each of his characteristic forms, the following should suffice:* Collected Poems, 1965 (*London*); Goodbye to All That (*autobiography; London, 1929; revised, 1957*); I, Claudius (*novel; London, 1934*); The White Goddess: A Historical Grammar of Poetic Myth (*London, 1948; revised, 1952*); Steps: Stories, Talks, Essays, Poems, Studies in History (*London, 1958*). *The first four of these are available in paperback reprints.*

CRITICAL WORKS AND COMMENTARY

Cohen, J. M. Robert Graves. Edinburgh and New York, 1960.
Day, Douglas. Swifter than Reason: The Poetry and Criticism of Robert Graves. Chapel Hill, N.C., 1963.
Fraser, G. S. "The Poetry of Robert Graves," in Vision and Rhetoric: Studies in Modern Poetry. London, 1959.
Jarrell, Randall. "Graves and the White Goddess," Parts I and II, *Yale Review*, XLV (Winter, Spring, 1956), 302–14, 467–78.
Seymour-Smith, Martin. Robert Graves. "Writers and Their Work," No. 78. London, 1956.
Spears, Monroe K. "The Latest Graves: Poet and Private Eye," *Sewanee Review*, LXXIII (Autumn, 1965), 660–78.